BUILD L♥VE

What You Do Matters!

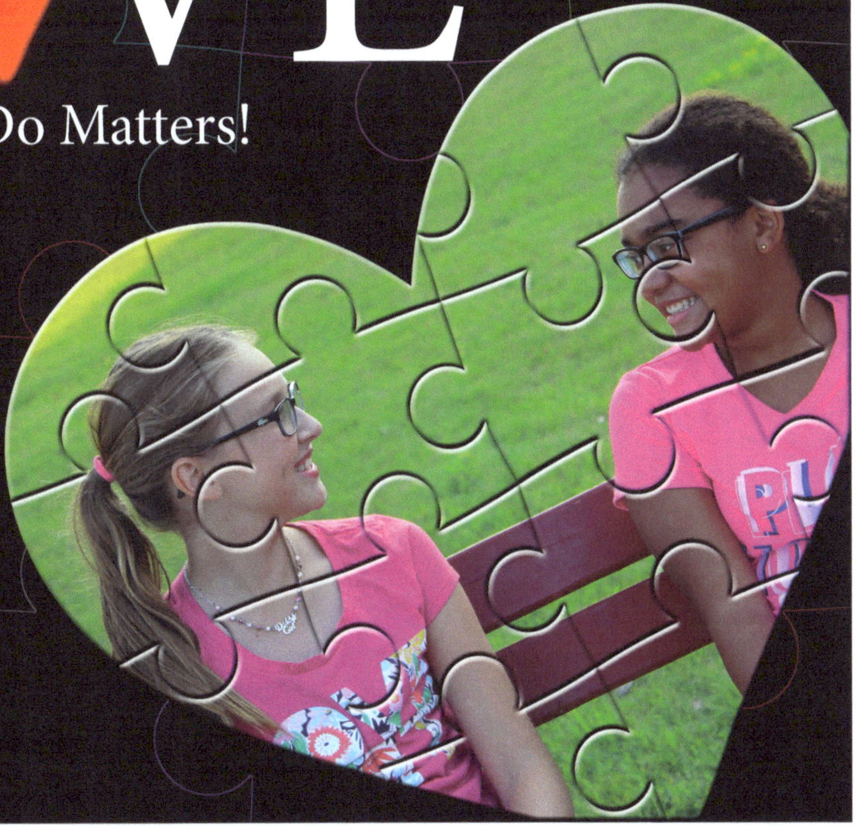

What You Do Matters!

No part of this publication may be reproduced in whole or in part, or stored in a retrieval system or transmitted in any form or by any means, electronic, mechanical, photocopying, recording, or otherwise, without written permission by the author. For information regarding permission, email Dr. Paula Henry at drpaulahenry@gmail.com.

ISBN 978-0-9893405-6-4
Library of Congress Control Number: 2018953862

Copyright © 2018 Dr. Paula Henry
All Rights Reserved

Publisher: How 2 Creative Services, 17550 200th Street, Audubon, MN 56511

Layout and design: Copyright © 2018, How 2 Creative Services of Audubon, MN

Photographs are credited to staff at Eastwood Elementary School, West Fargo, ND, particularly Kristi Kvernen, Jen Anderson, and Lisa Erickson and used with permission.

All children included in the photographs were used with parent permission.

All children included in the photographs were from Eastwood Elementary School, West Fargo, ND.

Thank you Mark and Sarah How for your support and encouragement.
You have blessed my life with your friendship.

This book is dedicated to my father, Harold Joseph Steil, who persevered through hardships over a lifetime. He taught me most about positivity, empathy, and love. I saw him demonstrate integrity and kindness daily.

How to use this book

As you read this book...
- Take time for discussion.
- Take time to read this over several days.
- Take time to brainstorm ideas and actions.
- Discuss what is important to children based on the ideas in this book.

Trees take a long time to grow. Children take time to grow.
Take time to build these ideas and actions with young people.

Vocabulary you will encounter in this book

- **Empathy** - the ability to understand and share the feelings of another.

- **Equity** – Taking extra measures by giving those who are in need more (care, support…) than others who are not, to ensure everyone's success in education and life.

"Never forget who you are."
(The Lion King)

"Everything you see exists together in a delicate balance."
Mufasa (The Lion King)

Interaction Institute for Social Change | Artist: Angus Maguire.

What is this book about?

Each of us can choose to make good things happen for other people through simple actions. What we do makes a difference and our actions are either positive, called "microaffirmations" or negative, called "microaggressions". We have the power to be kind and thoughtful and build love in our world.

This book will help you see that your choices make a difference. You will understand how your choices show who you really are.

"Build Love" is designed as a tool for adults to guide children in making good choices.

"Carry out a random act of kindness with no expectation of reward, safe in the knowledge that one day someone might do the same for you."
Princess Diana

Talk about these building blocks for love found in this book

- Empathy
- Self-Control
- Goodness
- Love
- Patience
- Kindness
- Gentleness
- Integrity
- Understanding
- Growth over time
- Character development
- Equity/Fairness
- Joy

How can you make a difference in others' lives?

What exactly are MICROAFFIRMATIONS?

- Small, subtle, kind behaviors
- Tiny actions showing caring and friendly behavior
- Listening, comforting, helping others
- Positive messages to others, intentional or unintentional
- Make people feel good about themselves

Microaffirmations are contagious. When you smile or compliment someone, he or she might smile at someone else. What YOU do matters to others.

Here are examples of how children define microaffirmations

This is a great activity to start conversations in the classroom, or at home about how we build love in our classroom, school, home, and community.

What microaffirmations do you see here?

1. _____
2. _____
3. _____

See page 35 for ideas.

"Do your little bit of good where you are; it's those little bits of good put together that overwhelm the world."
Archbishop Desmond Tutu

What exactly are MICROAGGRESSIONS?

- Small, subtle, hurtful behaviors
- Tiny actions that make others feel bad
- Everyday, verbal or nonverbal, slights, snubs, or insults, intentional or unintentional
- Negative messages
- Makes another person feel bad about themselves

Microaggressions are contagious. When you tease or say something mean to someone, he or she might be mean to someone else, or to you.

Here are examples of how children define microaggressions

This is a great activity to start conversations in the classroom or home about how we hurt others in our classroom, school, home, and community.

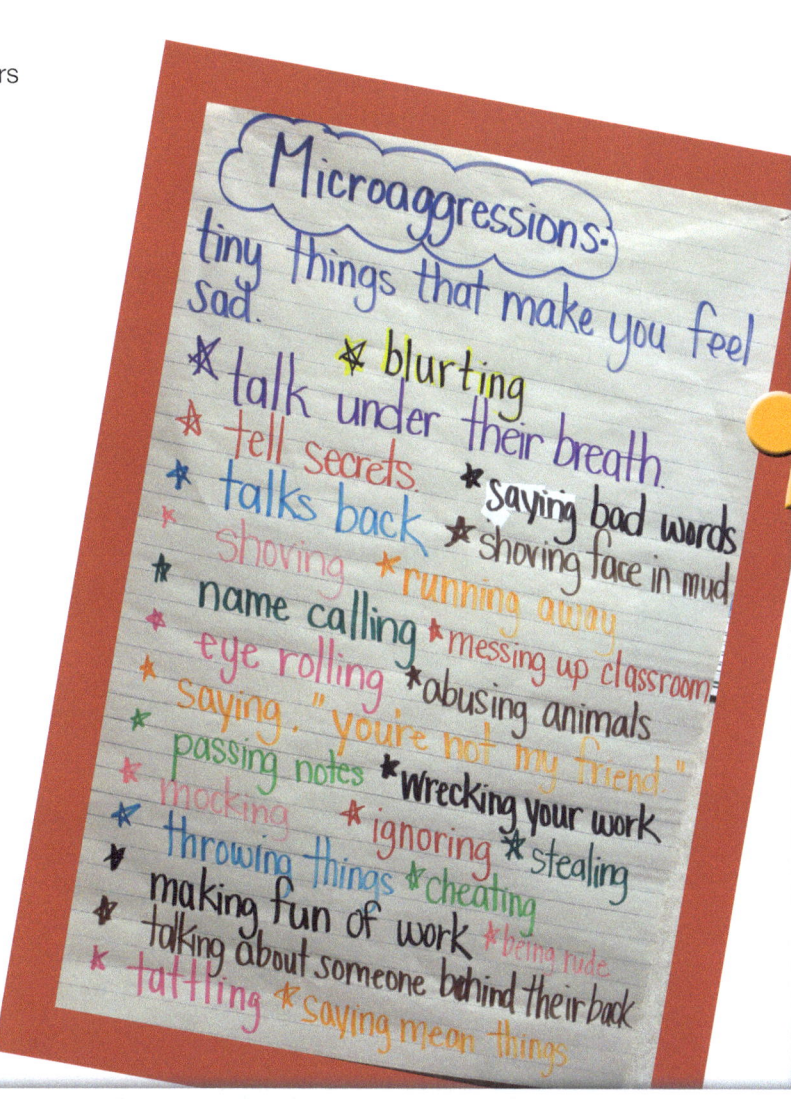

What microaggressions do you see here?

1. _____
2. _____
3. _____

See page 35 for ideas.

"Oh yes, the past can hurt. But, you can either run from it or, learn from it."
Mufasa (The Lion King)

CHOICES

Making Choices

Positive attitudes and thoughtful actions make your personal space - your classroom, school, home, and community - more enjoyable for everyone.

All day long we have moments of opportunity to make choices. It is important to make choices that are going to help you build positive connections with each other and build feelings of equity in others like belonging and significance, choices that help you build love.

This book will help you see what it looks like to make the right choices, stay on the positive side, and grow in empathy for others.

What actions make you feel good or bad?

Our bodies and brains respond to how we think and feel.
Small things that make us feel good or bad are powerful.

Microaffirmations – things that help people succeed – what makes us feel GOOD
- encouragement
- cheering
- hugs/kisses
- sharing
- high 5
- fair
- will you play with me
- smiles – wink
- pat on back
- paying attention to you
- nice note
- thumbs up
- kindness – Kind words
- helps you
- I'm proud of you
- please/thank you

Microaggressions – small things that make us feel BAD
- sticking out tongue
- ignoring
- hurt you (pushing)
- you're mean
- mean words
- frowning
- saying NO!
- rolls eyes
- copying you
- yells
- rude
- doesn't care
- teasing – name calling
- walks away
- I'm right
- bossy
- lying
- being sassy
- bullying
- laughing at you
- doing mean things

What small things do you see that matter here?

1. _____
2. _____
3. _____

See page 35 for ideas.

"It is vital that when educating our children's brains that we do not neglect their hearts."
Dali Lama

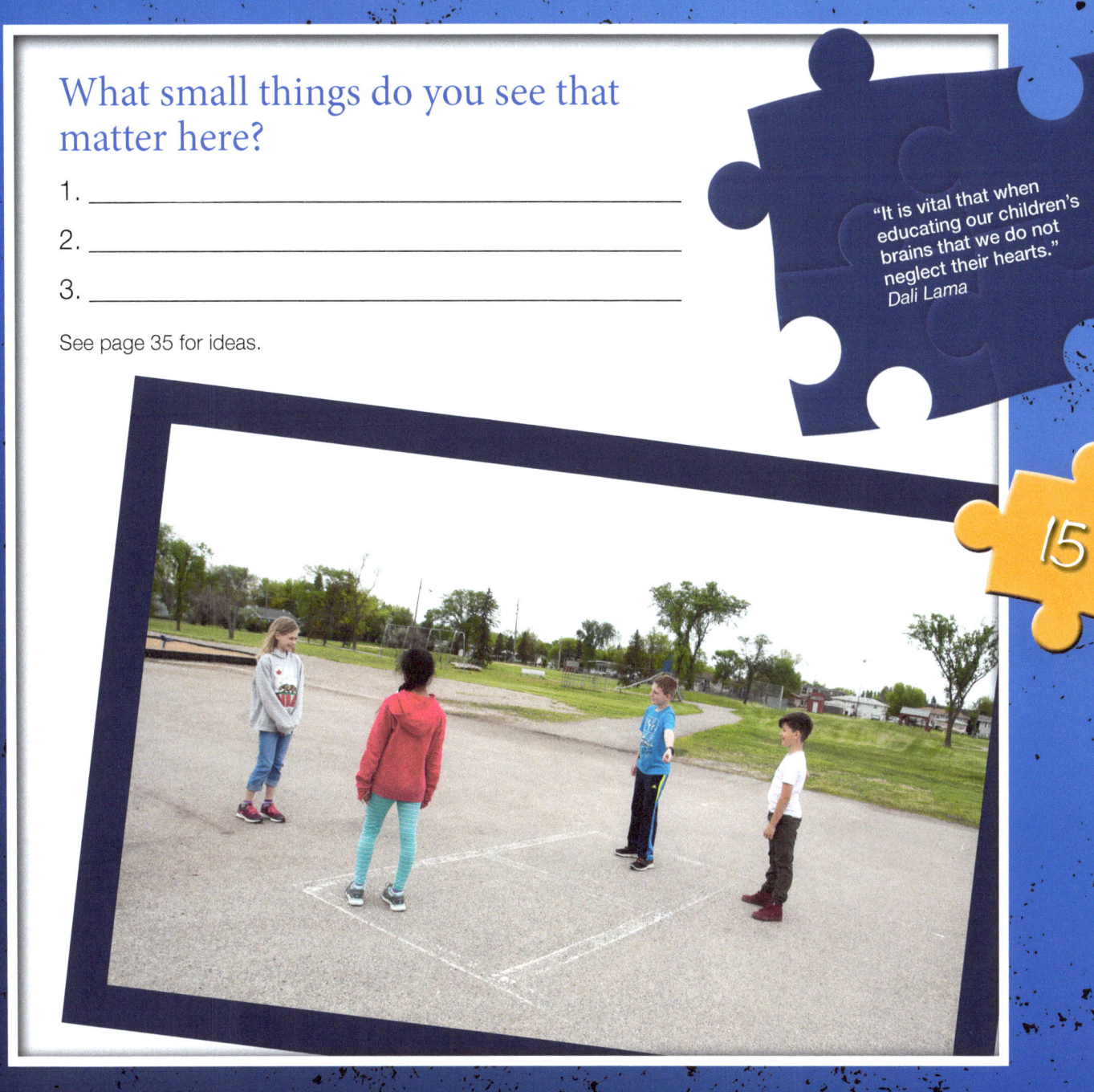

Why are your small actions important?

- Small actions matter
- You can make people happy
- You can inspire and lead through kindness
- You can create a sense of belonging and significance
- You can build a community of care and love
- You can make the world better

Be a positive part of someone's day. Show you care about what you do every moment. How can you be a happy part of someone's day?

You can build a sense of significance (make others feel important), belonging, and fun for everyone. You have that power. You can inspire and lead. You can build love.

Helping Others

You have the ability to help other kids' lives be happy and better. This can be a challenge.

Do be cheerful.
Do not be grumpy.

Do be empathetic.
Do not be judgmental.

Do be happy and kind.
Do not be hurtful.

You may have been hurt at one time. Use your experiences and feelings (empathy) to keep others from getting hurt.

Now, turn the page to see more about how YOU can make a difference in the world because YOU matter.

What microaffirmations do you see happening here?

1. _____
2. _____
3. _____

See page 35 for ideas.

"There are people who take the heart out of you, and there are people who put it back."
Elizabeth David

What microaggressions do you see here?

1. _____
2. _____
3. _____

See page 35 for ideas.

Today's secret is compassion. If we open our hearts to the way others feel we can help ease someone's pain.
Dali Lama

Let's understand microaffirmations and how they make you feel

What are the helpful or kind behaviors in this picture?

How do these small kind behaviors make you feel?

How would you feel if you would try to demonstrate (show) small acts of kindness in your school? In your community? In your home?

How do small acts of kindness build friendships in school, in your neighborhood, and community?

What is one thing you could do to build and strengthen friendships with small acts of kindness and thoughtfulness in your school, community, and home?

Let's understand microaggressions and how they make you feel

What are the hurtful behaviors in this picture?

How do these small hurtful behaviors make you feel?

How would you feel if you would try to stop these behaviors in your school? In your community? In your home?

How does stopping hurtful behaviors build friendships in school, in your neighborhood, and community?

What is one thing you could stop doing to build and strengthen friendships in your school, community, and home?

SCHOOL

MICROAFFIRMATIONS

What are the helpful or kind behaviors in this picture?

How do these small kind behaviors make you feel?

How can you try to demonstrate small acts of kindness in your school?

How do small acts of kindness build friendships in your school?

What is one thing you could do to build and strengthen friendships with small acts of kindness and thoughtfulness in your school?

MICROAGGRESSIONS

What are the hurtful behaviors in this picture?

How do these small hurtful behaviors make you feel?

How would you feel if you would try to stop these behaviors in your school?

How does stopping hurtful behaviors build friendships in schools?

What is one thing you could stop doing to build and strengthen friendships in your school?

HOME

MICROAFFIRMATIONS

What are the helpful or kind behaviors in this picture?

How do these small kind behaviors make you feel?

How can you try to demonstrate small acts of kindness in your home?

How do small acts of kindness build relationships in your home?

What is one thing you could do to build and strengthen friendships with small acts of kindness and thoughtfulness in your home?

MICROAGGRESSIONS

What are the hurtful behaviors in this picture?

How do these small hurtful behaviors make you feel?

How would you feel if you would try to stop these behaviors in your home?

How does stopping hurtful behaviors build relationships in your home?

What is one thing you could stop doing to build and strengthen relationships in your home?

NEIGHBORHOODS

MICROAFFIRMATIONS

What are the helpful or kind behaviors in this picture?

How do these small kind behaviors make you feel?

How can you try to demonstrate small acts of kindness in your neighborhood?

How do small acts of kindness build friendships in your neighborhood?

What is one thing you could do to build and strengthen friendships with small acts of kindness and thoughtfulness in your neighborhood?

MICROAGGRESSIONS

What are the hurtful behaviors in this picture?

How do these small hurtful behaviors make you feel?

How would you feel if you would try to stop these behaviors in your neighborhood?

How does stopping hurtful behaviors build friendships in your neighborhood?

What is one thing you could stop doing to build and strengthen friendships in your neighborhood?

COMMUNITY

MICROAFFIRMATIONS

What are the helpful or kind behaviors in this picture?

How do these small kind behaviors make you feel?

How can you try to demonstrate small acts of kindness in your community?

How do small acts of kindness build friendships in your community?

What is one thing you could do to build and strengthen friendships with small acts of kindness and thoughtfulness in your community?

MICROAGGRESSIONS

What are the hurtful behaviors in this picture?

How do these small hurtful behaviors make you feel?

How would you feel if you would try to stop these behaviors in your community?

How does stopping hurtful behaviors build friendships in your community?

What is one thing you could stop doing to build and strengthen friendships in your community?

WORLD

MICROAFFIRMATIONS

What are the helpful or kind behaviors in this picture?

How do these small kind behaviors make you feel?

How can you try to demonstrate small acts of kindness in your world?

How do small acts of kindness build friendships in your world?

What is one thing you could do to build and strengthen friendships with small acts of kindness and thoughtfulness in your world?

MICROAGGRESSIONS

What are the hurtful behaviors in this picture?

How do these small hurtful behaviors make you feel?

How would you feel if you would try to stop these behaviors in your world?

How does stopping hurtful behaviors build friendships in your world?

What is one thing you could stop doing to build and strengthen friendships in your world?

ACTION PLANS

So now that you know, what will you do today?

1. How can I help make good things happen for other people?
   - Smile. Smile with your bright eyes and your mouth.
   - (put your ideas here…)

2. How can I show care and empathy for others?
   - Be kind, attentive, approachable, and interested in others.
   - (put your ideas here…)

3. How can I show patience, kindness, and honesty?
   - Be nice to people, love people.
   - (put your ideas here…)

ACTION PLANS continued

Making a difference

We all have special abilities. What can you do to make a difference in your world?
Remember, we are all connected, we all matter, we all make a difference. It is your choice.

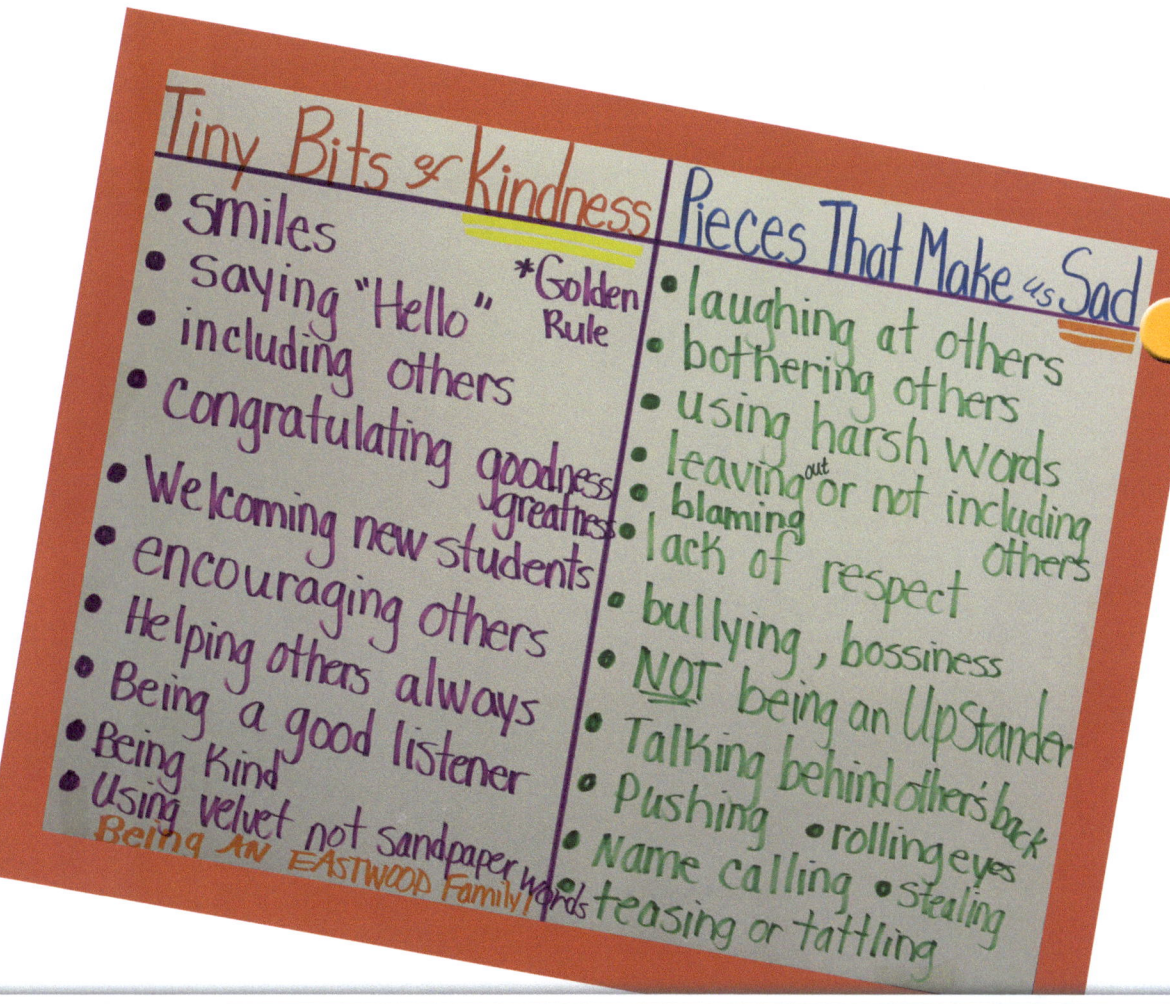

BUILD LOVE
What You Do Matters!

Be a happy part of someone's day!

34

KEY

What might you see?

Page 9
1. Smiling
2. Welcoming
3. Playing together

Page 12
1. Rolling eyes
2. Hands crossed
3. Not welcoming stance

Page 15
1. Welcoming
2. Showing where to stand
3. Smiling

Page 18
1. Helping
2. Giving attention
3. Smiling and being an up-stander

Page 19
1. Ignoring
2. Not giving help
3. No smiles or recognition

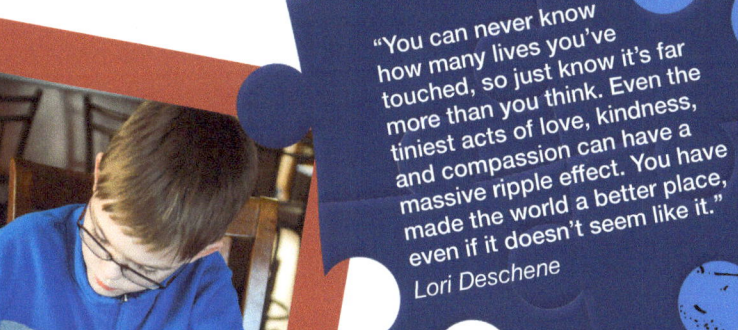

"You can never know how many lives you've touched, so just know it's far more than you think. Even the tiniest acts of love, kindness, and compassion can have a massive ripple effect. You have made the world a better place, even if it doesn't seem like it."
Lori Deschene

35

www.ingramcontent.com/pod-product-compliance
Lightning Source LLC
Chambersburg PA
CBHW041538040426
42446CB00002B/138